BLETCHLEY PARK

ONE MINUTE
PUZZLES

BLETCHLEYPARK

This edition was published in 2017 by the Bletchley Park Trust
The Mansion, Bletchley Park, Milton Keynes, MK3 6EB

Copyright © 2017 Arcturus Publishing Limited
Puzzles copyright © 2017 Puzzle Press Ltd

ISBN: 978-1-78828-041-9
AD005834NT

Cover design by Rose
Printed in the UK

CONTENTS

INTRODUCTION

During World War Two, Bletchley Park was a workplace to thousands of people whose job it was to read the encrypted messages of its enemies. Towards the end of 1941, a crossword puzzle competition was organised by the *Daily Telegraph*. The challenge was to complete the puzzle in under 12 minutes. A Mr Gavin, Chairman of the Eccentrics Club, offered to donate £100 to the Minesweepers Fund, if it could be done under controlled conditions. As a number of the competitors were subsequently invited to take part in intelligence work at Bletchley Park, puzzles and codebreaking have been linked in the public mind ever since the exploits of Bletchley Park's Codebreakers became public knowledge.

Codebreaking is very much a puzzle-solving process and the codes and ciphers used are similar to the most common types of puzzles such as crosswords, wordsearches and sudoku. In many cases, the Codebreakers of Bletchley Park were looking for patterns in the problem before them, much like puzzle solvers today. Both often also base their solutions on clues. For example, a simple code might represent words by something else such as strings of numbers. In this case, the clue may lie in the frequency of certain strings of numbers occurring in the encrypted message. Straight or quick crossword clues are simple definitions of the answers, so the clue lies in the definition provided. A more difficult cipher might replace each letter in a message with another letter of the alphabet twice, a so-called double-encryption. This is a bit like cryptic crosswords in which the clues are puzzles in themselves.

Encrypted World War Two enemy messages were usually transmitted in groups of letters, typically 4 or 5 in length. So when the letters were decrypted, they would still be in these letter groups but some letters might be missing. The Codebreakers would then have to piece the actual words of the message together. This is a bit like a 'fill-in-the-blank' clue in crosswords or wordsearch puzzles.

So you see, puzzle solving is synonymous with the profound intellectual feat and remarkable brains of those whose work at Bletchley Park is said to have helped shorten World War Two by up to two years. Following in this long-held tradition, the Bletchley Park Trust has today produced this series of puzzle books so that you can follow in the footsteps of the Codebreakers and perhaps establish whether you have the puzzle-solving skills needed to have worked at wartime Bletchley Park...

1

One to Nine *WITHOUT BODMAS*

Using the numbers below, complete these six equations
(three reading across and three reading downwards).
Every number is used once.

$$1 \quad 2 \quad 3$$

$$4 \quad 5 \quad 6$$

$$7 \quad 8 \quad 9$$

4	x	6	–	9	=	15
+		x		+		
8	–	1	x	3	=	21
–		+		x		
2	x	5	+	7	=	17
=		=		=		
10		11		84		

6

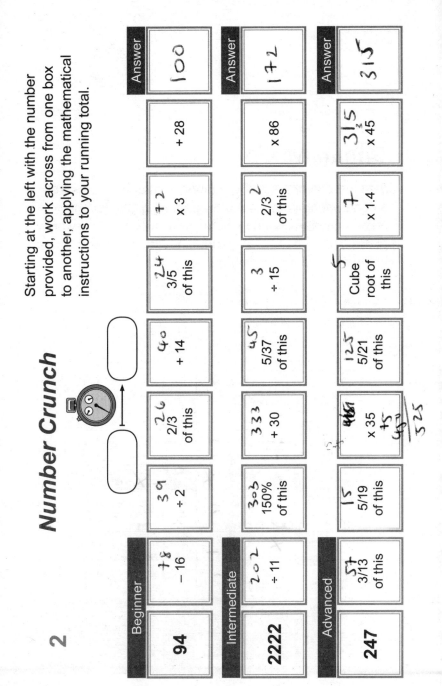

Number Crunch

Starting at the left with the number provided, work across from one box to another, applying the mathematical instructions to your running total.

2

Beginner

94	– 16	÷ 2	2/3 of this	+ 14	3/5 of this	× 3	+ 28	Answer
	78	*39*	*26*	*40*	*24*	*72*		*100*

Intermediate

2222	÷ 11	150% of this	+ 30	5/37 of this	÷ 15	2/3 of this	× 86	Answer
	202	*303*	*333*	*45*	*3*	*2*		*172*

Advanced

247	3/13 of this	5/19 of this	× 35	5/21 of this	Cube root of this	× 1.4	× 45	Answer
	57	*15*	*525*	*125*	*5*	*7*	*315*	*315*

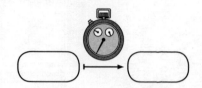

Summing Up

Arrange one of each of the four given numbers, as well as one each of the symbols – (minus), x (times) and + (plus) in every row and column to arrive at the answer at the end of the row or column, making the calculations in the order in which they appear.

2   3

7   8

3	+	8	x	2	–	7	=	15
=		–		+		+		
2	+	7	–	3	×	8	=	48
+		+		×		×		
7	–	3	+	8	×	2	=	24
×		×		–		–		
8	×	2	–	7	+	3	=	12
=		=		=		=		
64		8		33		27		

8

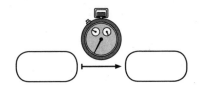

Isolate

Draw walls to partition the grid into areas (some walls are already drawn in for you). Each area must contain two circles, area sizes must match those shown by the numbers next to the grid and each '+' must be linked to at least two walls.

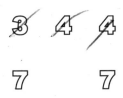

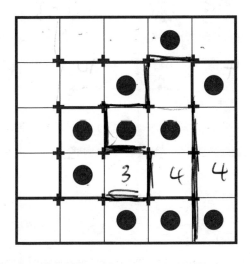

5

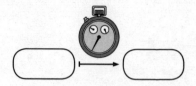

Pyramid Plus

The number in each circle is the sum of the two numbers below it. Just work out the missing numbers in every circle!

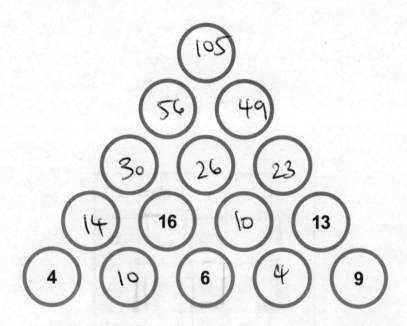

6

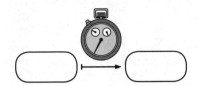

One to Nine

Using the numbers below, complete these six equations (three reading across and three reading downwards). Every number is used once.

1 2 3

4 5 6

7 8 9

8	–	1	x	5	= 35
+		+		x	
2	x	9	+	3	= 21
–		x		+	
4	x	6	–	7	= 17
=		=		=	
6		60		22	

11

Number Crunch

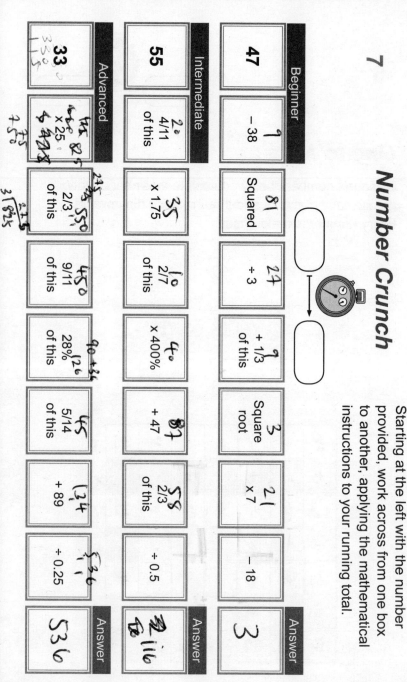

Starting at the left with the number provided, work across from one box to another, applying the mathematical instructions to your running total.

Beginner

47 | −38 | Squared | ÷ 3 | + 1/3 of this | Square root | × 7 | − 18 | **Answer** 3

Intermediate

55 | 4/11 of this | × 1.75 | 2/7 of this | × 400% | + 47 | 2/3 of this | ÷ 0.5 | **Answer**

Advanced

33 | × 25 | 2/3 of this | 9/11 of this | 28% of this | 5/14 of this | + 89 | + 0.25 | **Answer** 536

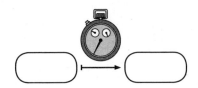

Summing Up

Arrange one of each of the four given numbers, as well as one each of the symbols – (minus), x (times) and + (plus) in every row and column to arrive at the answer at the end of the row or column, making the calculations in the order in which they appear.

3 5

6 9

5	+	9	x	3	–	6	=	36
–		X		X		+		
3	x	5	–	6	+	9	=	18
X		–		+		X		
9	+	6	X	5	–	3	=	72
+		+		–		–		
6	–	3	X	9	+	5	=	32
=		=		=		=		
24		42		14		40		

Isolate

Draw walls to partition the grid into areas (some walls are already drawn in for you). Each area must contain two circles, area sizes must match those shown by the numbers next to the grid and each '+' must be linked to at least two walls.

~~2~~ ~~3~~ ~~3~~ ~~3~~

~~4~~ ~~5~~ ~~5~~

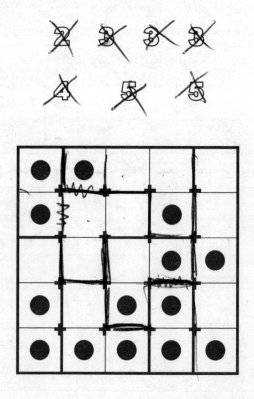

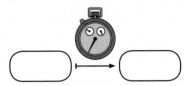

Pyramid Plus

The number in each circle is the sum of the two numbers below it. Just work out the missing numbers in every circle!

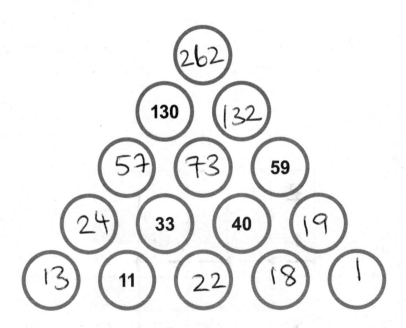

One to Nine

Using the numbers below, complete these six equations (three reading across and three reading downwards). Every number is used once.

$$1 \quad 2 \quad 3$$
$$4 \quad 5 \quad 6$$
$$7 \quad 8 \quad 9$$

2	+	7	−	5	=	4
+		−		x		
6	x	3	−	8	=	10
x		+		−		
9	−	1	x	4	=	32
=		=		=		
72		5		36		

Number Crunch

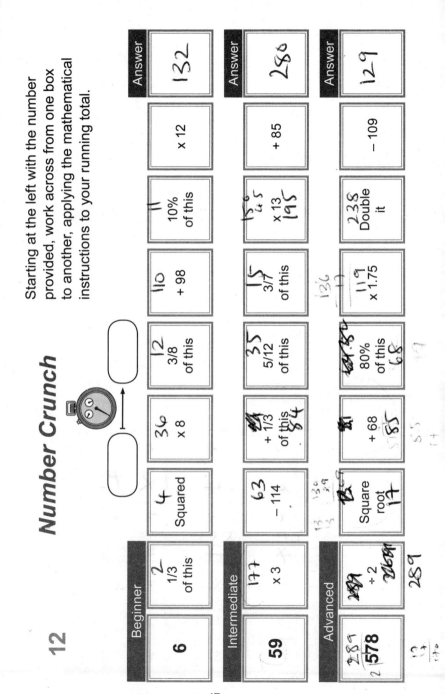

Starting at the left with the number provided, work across from one box to another, applying the mathematical instructions to your running total.

12

Beginner

| 6 | 2 1/3 of this | 4 Squared | 36 x 8 | 12 3/8 of this | 110 + 98 | 11 10% of this | x 12 | Answer 132 |

Intermediate

| 59 | 177 x 3 | 63 − 114 | 44 + 1/3 of this 94 | 35 5/12 of this | 15 3/7 of this | 155 45 x 13 195 | + 85 | Answer 288 |

Advanced

| 578 ÷ 2 | 289 ÷ 2 269 | Square root 17 | 31 + 68 155 | 85 80% of this 68 | 119 x 1.75 | 238 Double it | − 109 | Answer 129 |

13 3
130 39
136
289
55

Summing Up

Arrange one of each of the four given numbers, as well
as one each of the symbols – (minus), x (times) and +
(plus) in every row and column to arrive at the answer
at the end of the row or column, making the calculations
in the order in which they appear.

4 6

7 9

6	x	9	–	4	+	7	=	57
–		+		X		–		
4	+	7	–	9	X	6	=	12
X		–		–		X		
7	–	4	X	6	+	9	=	27
+		X		+		+		
9	+	6	–	7	X	4	=	32
=		=		=		=		
23		72		37		13		

14

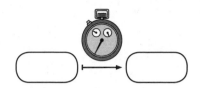

Isolate

Draw walls to partition the grid into areas (some walls are already drawn in for you). Each area must contain two circles, area sizes must match those shown by the numbers next to the grid and each '+' must be linked to at least two walls.

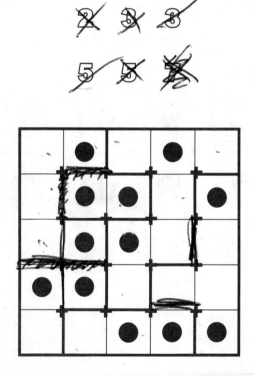

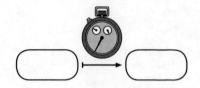

Pyramid Plus

The number in each circle is the sum of the two numbers below it. Just work out the missing numbers in every circle!

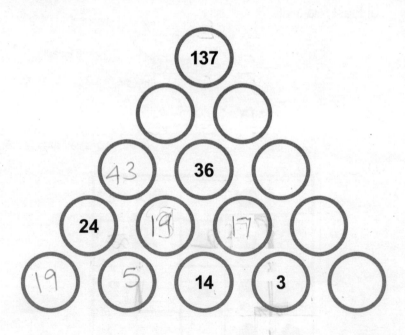

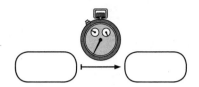

One to Nine

Using the numbers below, complete these six equations
(three reading across and three reading downwards).
Every number is used once.

1   2   3

4   5   6

7   8   9

	+	4	x		=	63
−		x		+		
	x		−		=	26
x		+		x		
	x		+		=	20
=		=		=		
4		42		64		

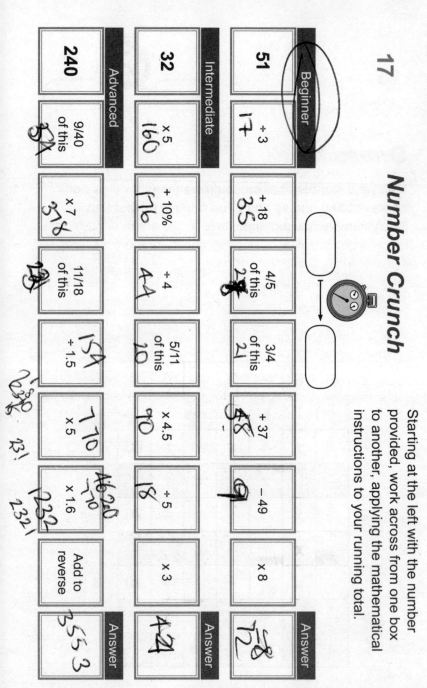

17

Number Crunch

Starting at the left with the number provided, work across from one box to another, applying the mathematical instructions to your running total.

Beginner

51	÷ 3	+ 18	4/5 of this	3/4 of this	+ 37	− 49	× 8	Answer

Handwritten: 17, 35, 28, 21, 48, 9, 72/78

Intermediate

32	× 5	+ 10%	÷ 4	5/11 of this	× 4.5	÷ 5	× 3	Answer

Handwritten: 160, 176, 44, 20, 90, 18, 424

Advanced

240	9/40 of this	× 7	11/18 of this	+ 1.5	× 5	× 1.6	Add to reverse	Answer

Handwritten: 54, 378, 231, 154, 770, 1620, 232, 3553

22

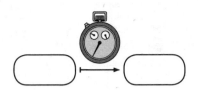

Summing Up

Arrange one of each of the four given numbers, as well as one each of the symbols – (minus), x (times) and + (plus) in every row and column to arrive at the answer at the end of the row or column, making the calculations in the order in which they appear.

2   4

5   8

2	+	8	x	5	–	4	=	46
x		–		–		+		
5	x	4	–	2	+	8	=	26
–		x		x		x		
4	+	2	x	8	–	5	=	43
+		x		+		–		
8	x	5	+	4	–	2	=	42
=		=		=		=		
14		30		28		58		

19

Isolate

Draw walls to partition the grid into areas (some walls are already drawn in for you). Each area must contain two circles, area sizes must match those shown by the numbers next to the grid and each '+' must be linked to at least two walls.

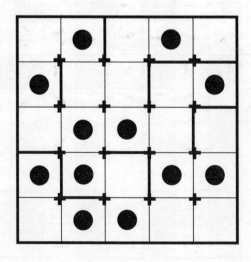

20

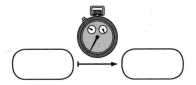

Pyramid Plus

The number in each circle is the sum of the two numbers below it. Just work out the missing numbers in every circle!

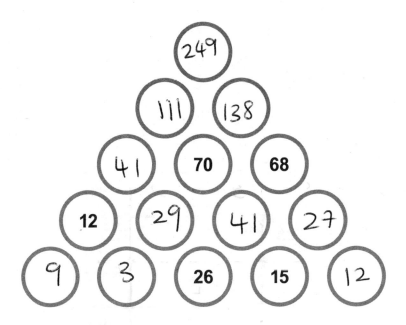

One to Nine

Using the numbers below, complete these six equations (three reading across and three reading downwards). Every number is used once.

1   2   3

4   5   6

7   8   9

8	x	3	+	6	=	30
-		+		x		
5	+	2	x	7	=	49
+		x		-		
1	+	9	x	4	=	40
=		=		=		
4		45		38		

26

Number Crunch

Starting at the left with the number provided, work across from one box to another, applying the mathematical instructions to your running total.

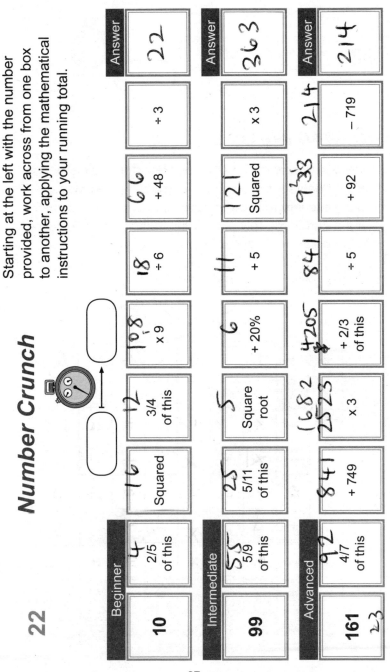

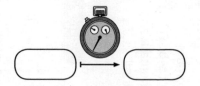

Summing Up

Arrange one of each of the four given numbers, as well as one each of the symbols – (minus), x (times) and + (plus) in every row and column to arrive at the answer at the end of the row or column, making the calculations in the order in which they appear.

3   6

7   9

3	+	7	–	9	x	6	=	6
x		–		+		x		
9	–	3	x	6	+	7	=	43
+		x		–		–		
6	x	9	+	7	–	3	=	58
–		+		x		+		
7	–	6	+	3	x	9	=	36
=		=		=		=		
26		42		24		48		

24

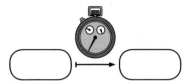

Isolate

Draw walls to partition the grid into areas (some walls are already drawn in for you). Each area must contain two circles, area sizes must match those shown by the numbers next to the grid and each '+' must be linked to at least two walls.

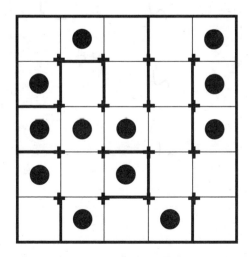

Pyramid Plus

The number in each circle is the sum of the two numbers below it. Just work out the missing numbers in every circle!

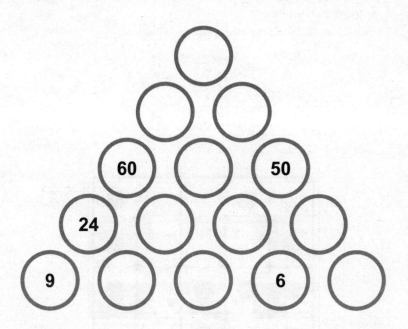

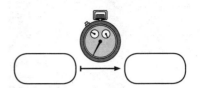

One to Nine

Using the numbers below, complete these six equations (three reading across and three reading downwards). Every number is used once.

$$1 \quad 2 \quad 3$$

$$4 \quad 5 \quad 6$$

$$7 \quad 8 \quad 9$$

	+	2	x		=	30
+		x		−		
	+		−		=	12
−		+		x		
	−		x		=	49
=		=		=		
2		19		14		

Number Crunch

Starting at the left with the number provided, work across from one box to another, applying the mathematical instructions to your running total.

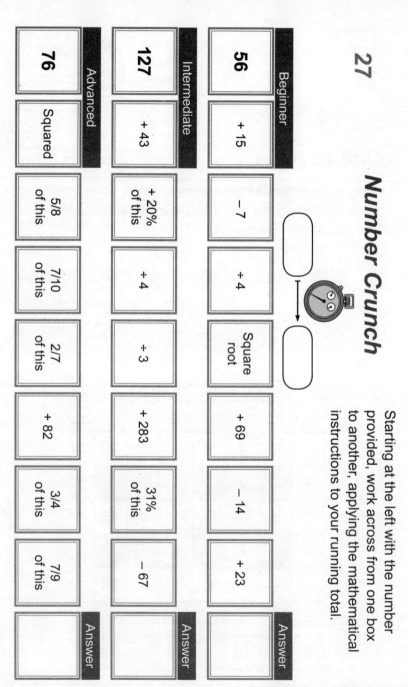

Beginner

56	+ 15	− 7	÷ 4	Square root	+ 69	− 14	+ 23	Answer

Intermediate

127	+ 43	+ 20% of this	÷ 4	÷ 3	+ 283	31% of this	− 67	Answer

Advanced

76	Squared	5/8 of this	7/10 of this	2/7 of this	+ 82	3/4 of this	7/9 of this	Answer

Summing Up

Arrange one of each of the four given numbers, as well as one each of the symbols – (minus), x (times) and + (plus) in every row and column to arrive at the answer at the end of the row or column, making the calculations in the order in which they appear.

3 4

6 8

6	+	4	x	8	–	3	=	77
							=	26
x								
	–				+		=	14
			3				=	44
=		=		=		=		
20		30		27		22		

Isolate

Draw walls to partition the grid into areas (some walls are already drawn in for you). Each area must contain two circles, area sizes must match those shown by the numbers next to the grid and each '+' must be linked to at least two walls.

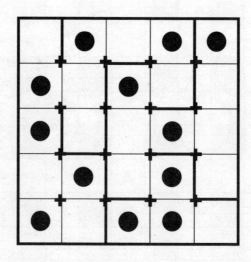

30

Pyramid Plus

The number in each circle is the sum of the two numbers below it. Just work out the missing numbers in every circle!

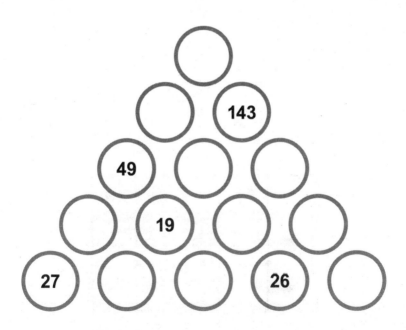

One to Nine

Using the numbers below, complete these six equations (three reading across and three reading downwards). Every number is used once.

1 2 3

4 5 6

7 8 9

	−		x		=	8
+		x		+		
1	+		x		=	36
x		+		x		
	x		−		=	33
=		=		=		
45		25		26		

32

Number Crunch

Starting at the left with the number provided, work across from one box to another, applying the mathematical instructions to your running total.

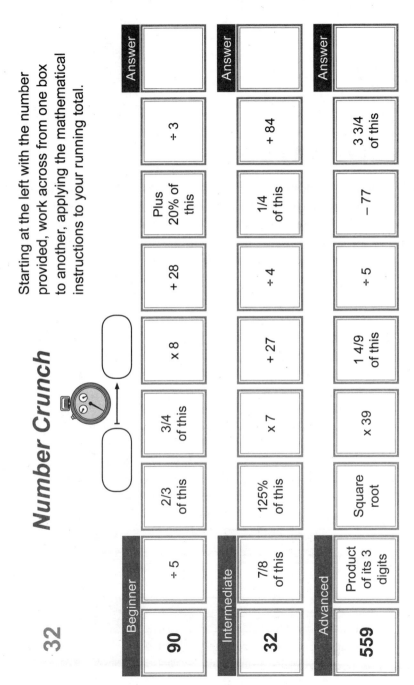

Beginner

| 90 | ÷ 5 | 2/3 of this | 3/4 of this | × 8 | + 28 | Plus 20% of this | ÷ 3 | Answer |

Intermediate

| 32 | 7/8 of this | 125% of this | × 7 | + 27 | ÷ 4 | 1/4 of this | + 84 | Answer |

Advanced

| 559 | Product of its 3 digits | Square root | × 39 | 1 4/9 of this | ÷ 5 | − 77 | 3 3/4 of this | Answer |

37

Summing Up

Arrange one of each of the four given numbers, as well as one each of the symbols – (minus), x (times) and + (plus) in every row and column to arrive at the answer at the end of the row or column, making the calculations in the order in which they appear.

2 5

7 9

5	+	9	x	2	–	7	=	21
							=	12
				9			=	50
					x		=	22
=		=		=		=		
90		15		76		78		

34

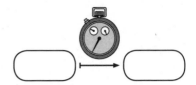

Isolate

Draw walls to partition the grid into areas (some walls
are already drawn in for you). Each area must contain
two circles, area sizes must match those shown by the
numbers next to the grid and each '+' must be linked to
at least two walls.

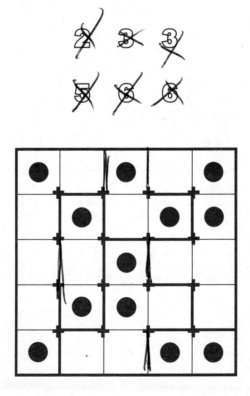

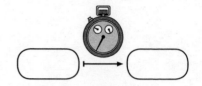

Pyramid Plus

The number in each circle is the sum of the two numbers below it. Just work out the missing numbers in every circle!

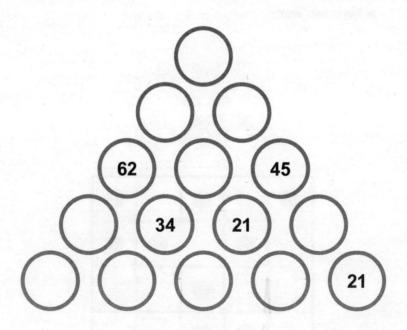

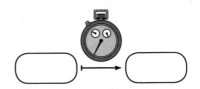

One to Nine

Using the numbers below, complete these six equations (three reading across and three reading downwards). Every number is used once.

1 2 3

4 5 6

7 8 9

	–	3	x		=	48
+		x		–		
	+		x		=	40
x		–		x		
	+		–		=	10
=		=		=		
77		14		3		

Number Crunch

Starting at the left with the number provided, work across from one box to another, applying the mathematical instructions to your running total.

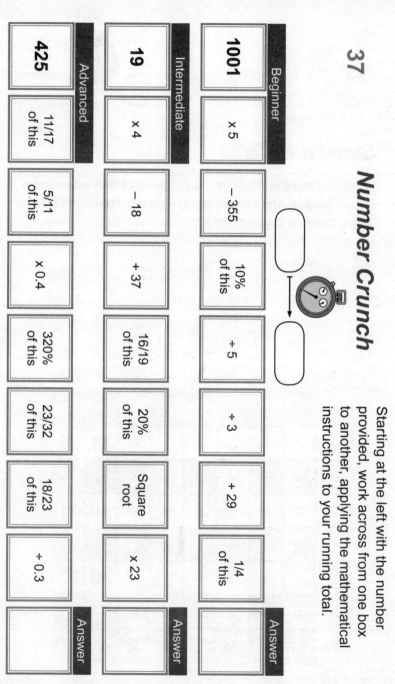

Beginner

| 1001 | × 5 | − 355 | 10% of this | ÷ 5 | ÷ 3 | + 29 | 1/4 of this | Answer |

Intermediate

| 19 | × 4 | − 18 | + 37 | 16/19 of this | 20% of this | Square root | × 23 | Answer |

Advanced

| 425 | 11/17 of this | 5/11 of this | × 0.4 | 320% of this | 23/32 of this | 18/23 of this | ÷ 0.3 | Answer |

Summing Up

Arrange one of each of the four given numbers, as well as one each of the symbols – (minus), x (times) and + (plus) in every row and column to arrive at the answer at the end of the row or column, making the calculations in the order in which they appear.

3   4

7   8

4	+	7	x	3	–	8	=	25
				7			=	39
	x				+		=	11
			+				=	57
=		=		=		=		
36		24		76		33		

39

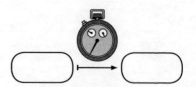

Isolate

Draw walls to partition the grid into areas (some walls are already drawn in for you). Each area must contain two circles, area sizes must match those shown by the numbers next to the grid and each '+' must be linked to at least two walls.

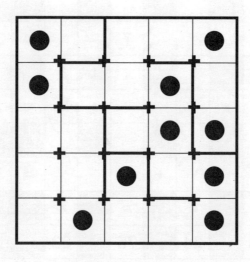

40

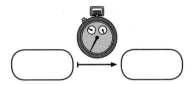

Pyramid Plus

The number in each circle is the sum of the two numbers below it. Just work out the missing numbers in every circle!

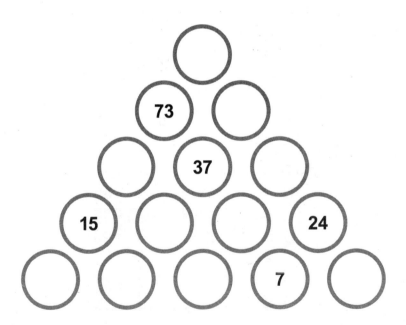

One to Nine

Using the numbers below, complete these six equations (three reading across and three reading downwards). Every number is used once.

1　2　3

4　5　6

7　8　9

	+		x		=	35
x		+		−		
	+		−		=	12
−		x		+		
3	x		+		=	24
=		=		=		
21		45		14		

Number Crunch

Starting at the left with the number provided, work across from one box to another, applying the mathematical instructions to your running total.

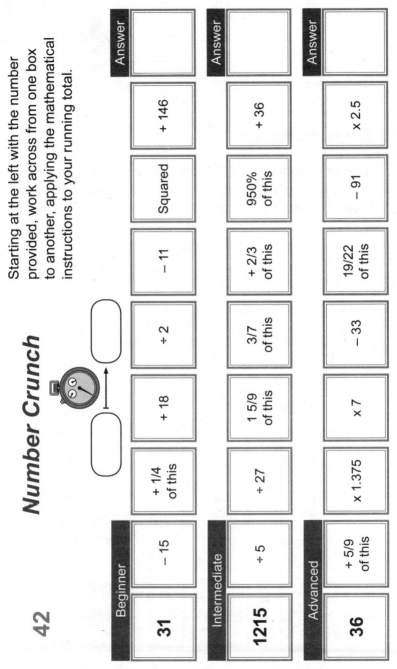

Beginner								Answer
31	− 15	+ 1/4 of this	+ 18	÷ 2	− 11	Squared	+ 146	

Intermediate								Answer
1215	÷ 5	÷ 27	1 5/9 of this	3/7 of this	+ 2/3 of this	950% of this	+ 36	

Advanced								Answer
36	+ 5/9 of this	x 1.375	x 7	− 33	19/22 of this	− 91	x 2.5	

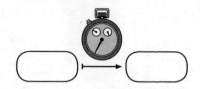

Summing Up

Arrange one of each of the four given numbers, as well as one each of the symbols – (minus), x (times) and + (plus) in every row and column to arrive at the answer at the end of the row or column, making the calculations in the order in which they appear.

$$2 \quad 5$$

$$6 \quad 8$$

5	x	8	+	2	–	6	=	36
						=	28	
	–				x		=	18
						–		
				8			=	59
=		=		=		=		
86		66		12		23		

48

44

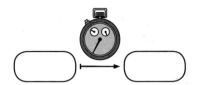

Isolate

Draw walls to partition the grid into areas (some walls are already drawn in for you). Each area must contain two circles, area sizes must match those shown by the numbers next to the grid and each '+' must be linked to at least two walls.

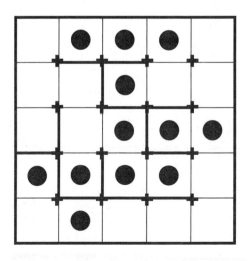

49

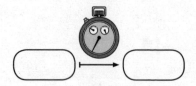

Pyramid Plus

The number in each circle is the sum of the two numbers below it. Just work out the missing numbers in every circle!

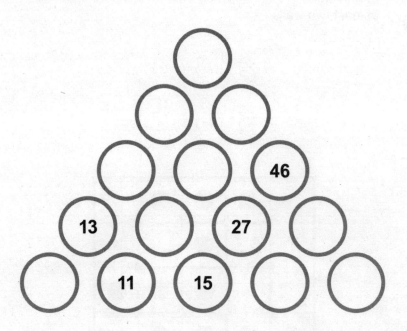

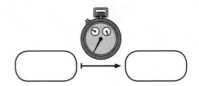

One to Nine

Using the numbers below, complete these six equations (three reading across and three reading downwards). Every number is used once.

1   ~~2~~   3

4   5   6

7   8   ~~9~~

3 ~~6 1 2 4~~ ³	x	6 ~~9 3 16~~	−	9	=	9
+		−		+		
2²	+	5⁵	x	7	=	49
x		x		x		
8⁸	−	1	+	4	=	11
=		=		=		
40		1		64		

Number Crunch

Starting at the left with the number provided, work across from one box to another, applying the mathematical instructions to your running total.

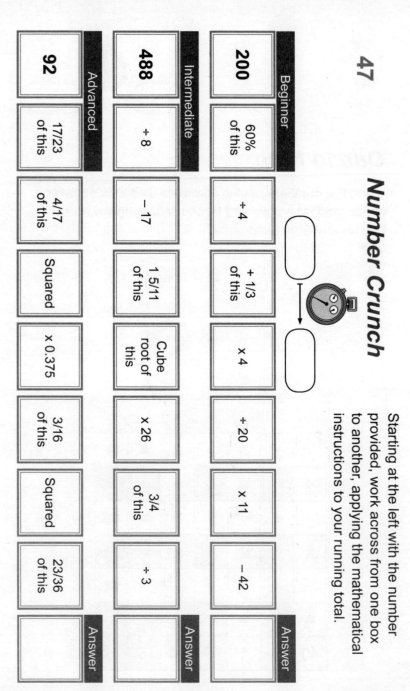

Beginner

| 200 | 60% of this | ÷ 4 | + 1/3 of this | × 4 | ÷ 20 | × 11 | − 42 | Answer |

Intermediate

| 488 | ÷ 8 | − 17 | 1 5/11 of this | Cube root of this | × 26 | 3/4 of this | ÷ 3 | Answer |

Advanced

| 92 | 17/23 of this | 4/17 of this | Squared | × 0.375 | 3/16 of this | Squared | 23/36 of this | Answer |

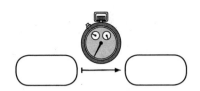

Summing Up

Arrange one of each of the four given numbers, as well as one each of the symbols – (minus), x (times) and + (plus) in every row and column to arrive at the answer at the end of the row or column, making the calculations in the order in which they appear.

2   5

7   9

5	+	7	–	2	x	9	=	90
						–		
						=	12	
			7	+		=	54	
					x			
						=	78	
=		=		=		=		
34		15		16		14		

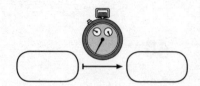

Isolate

Draw walls to partition the grid into areas (some walls are already drawn in for you). Each area must contain two circles, area sizes must match those shown by the numbers next to the grid and each '+' must be linked to at least two walls.

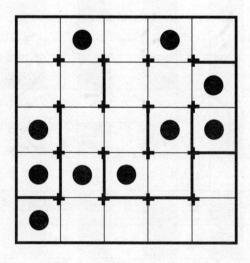

50

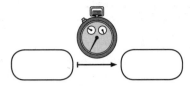

Pyramid Plus

The number in each circle is the sum of the two
numbers below it. Just work out the missing numbers in
every circle!

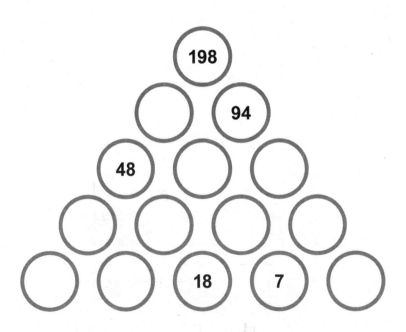

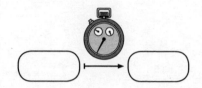

One to Nine

Using the numbers below, complete these six equations (three reading across and three reading downwards). Every number is used once.

1 2 3

4 5 6

7 8 9

	+		x		=	10
x		–		+		
	–		x		=	9
+		x		x		
	x	4	+		=	34
=		=		=		
26		8		20		

Number Crunch

Starting at the left with the number provided, work across from one box to another, applying the mathematical instructions to your running total.

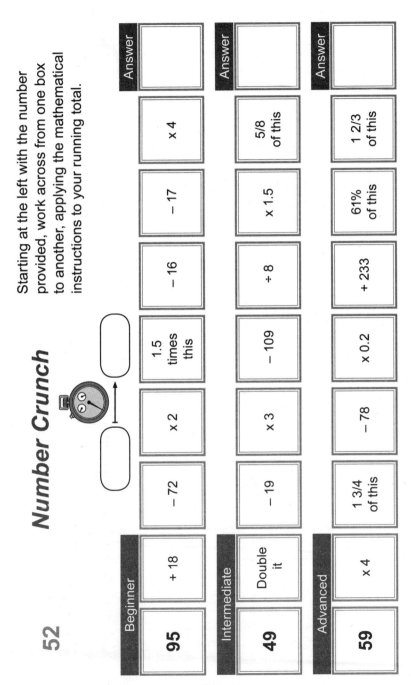

Beginner

| 95 | + 18 | − 72 | × 2 | 1.5 times this | − 16 | − 17 | × 4 | Answer |

Intermediate

| 49 | Double it | − 19 | × 3 | − 109 | ÷ 8 | × 1.5 | 5/8 of this | Answer |

Advanced

| 59 | × 4 | 1 3/4 of this | − 78 | × 0.2 | + 233 | 61% of this | 1 2/3 of this | Answer |

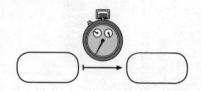

53

Summing Up

Arrange one of each of the four given numbers, as well
as one each of the symbols – (minus), x (times) and +
(plus) in every row and column to arrive at the answer
at the end of the row or column, making the calculations
in the order in which they appear.

$$3 \quad 5$$
$$7 \quad 8$$

5	–	3	+	8	x	7	=	70
		x						
							=	30
							=	26
	–		x				=	14
=		=		=		=		
32		18		24		40		

54

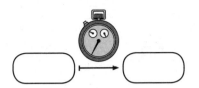

Isolate

Draw walls to partition the grid into areas (some walls are already drawn in for you). Each area must contain two circles, area sizes must match those shown by the numbers next to the grid and each '+' must be linked to at least two walls.

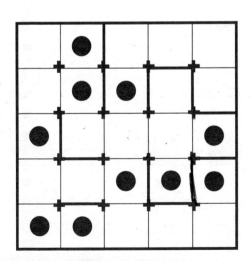

Pyramid Plus

The number in each circle is the sum of the two numbers below it. Just work out the missing numbers in every circle!

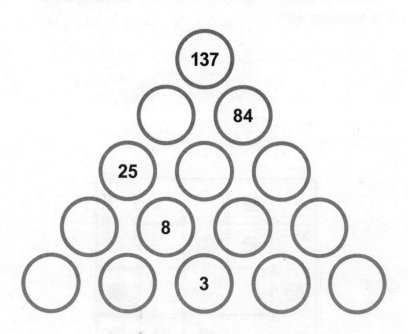

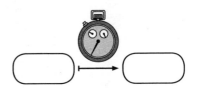

One to Nine

Using the numbers below, complete these six equations
(three reading across and three reading downwards).
Every number is used once.

1 2 3

4 5 6

7 8 9

	x		–		=	30
x		+		–		
3	+		x		=	10
+		–		+		
	–		x		=	6
=		=		=		
20		11		7		

Number Crunch

Starting at the left with the number provided, work across from one box to another, applying the mathematical instructions to your running total.

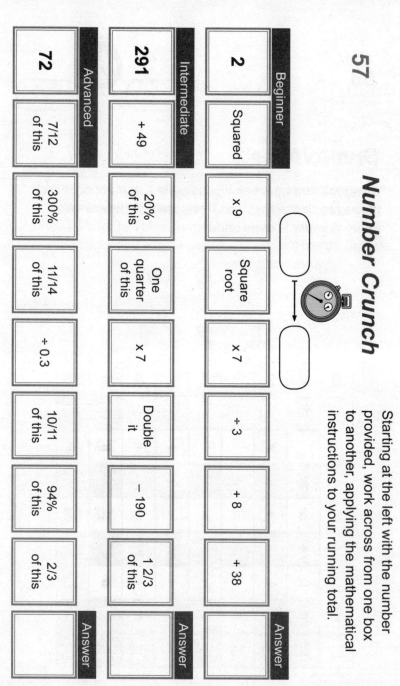

Beginner

| 2 | Squared | x 9 | Square root | x 7 | ÷ 3 | + 8 | + 38 | Answer |

Intermediate

| 291 | + 49 | 20% of this | One quarter of this | x 7 | Double it | – 190 | 1 2/3 of this | Answer |

Advanced

| 72 | 7/12 of this | 300% of this | 11/14 of this | ÷ 0.3 | 10/11 of this | 94% of this | 2/3 of this | Answer |

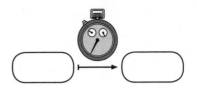

Summing Up

Arrange one of each of the four given numbers, as well as one each of the symbols – (minus), x (times) and + (plus) in every row and column to arrive at the answer at the end of the row or column, making the calculations in the order in which they appear.

9	–	3	+	1	x	8	=	56
					+		=	4
							=	98
					x			
	–						=	90
=		=		=		=		
22		20		78		54		

Isolate

Draw walls to partition the grid into areas (some walls are already drawn in for you). Each area must contain two circles, area sizes must match those shown by the numbers next to the grid and each '+' must be linked to at least two walls.

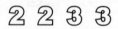

2 2 3 3

5 5 5

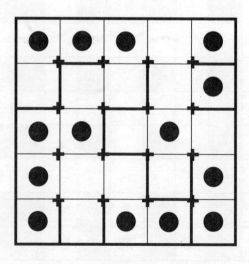

60

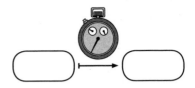

Pyramid Plus

The number in each circle is the sum of the two numbers below it. Just work out the missing numbers in every circle!

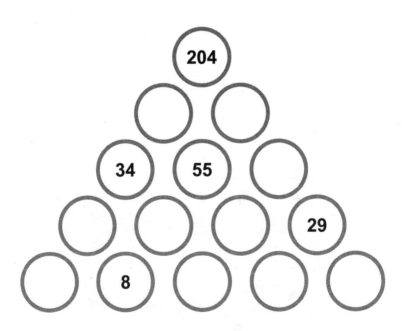

One to Nine

Using the numbers below, complete these six equations (three reading across and three reading downwards). Every number is used once.

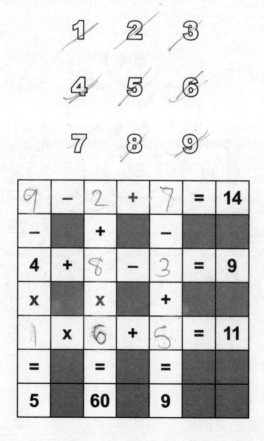

9	−	2	+	7	=	14
−		+		−		
4	+	8	−	3	=	9
x		x		+		
1	x	6	+	5	=	11
=		=		=		
5		60		9		

Number Crunch

Starting at the left with the number provided, work across from one box to another, applying the mathematical instructions to your running total.

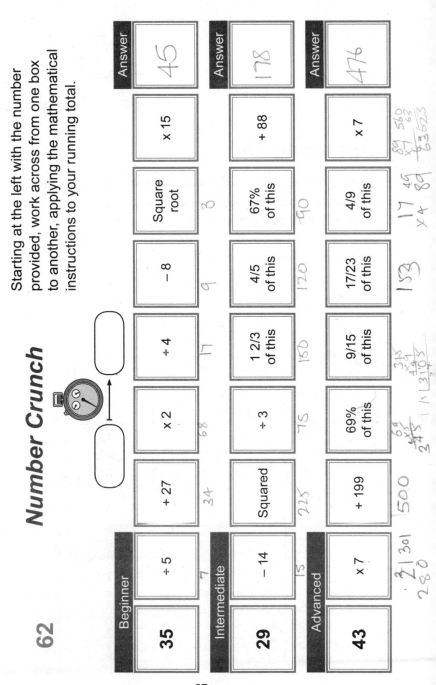

Beginner							Answer
35	÷ 5	+ 27	x 2	÷ 4	– 8	Square root	x 15	45

Intermediate							Answer
29	– 14	Squared	÷ 3	69% of this	1 2/3 of this	4/5 of this	67% of this	+ 88	178

Advanced							Answer
43	x 7	+ 199	69% of this	9/15 of this	17/23 of this	4/9 of this	x 7	476

Summing Up

Arrange one of each of the four given numbers, as well as one each of the symbols – (minus), x (times) and + (plus) in every row and column to arrive at the answer at the end of the row or column, making the calculations in the order in which they appear.

2   3

5   7

3	x	7	–	5	+	2	=	18
							=	24
x								
			x			7	=	14
				+				
							=	15
=		=		=		=		
9		28		34		30		

64

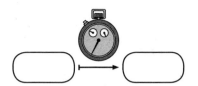

Isolate

Draw walls to partition the grid into areas (some walls are already drawn in for you). Each area must contain two circles, area sizes must match those shown by the numbers next to the grid and each '+' must be linked to at least two walls.

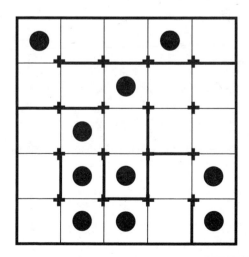

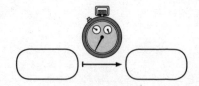

Pyramid Plus

The number in each circle is the sum of the two numbers below it. Just work out the missing numbers in every circle!

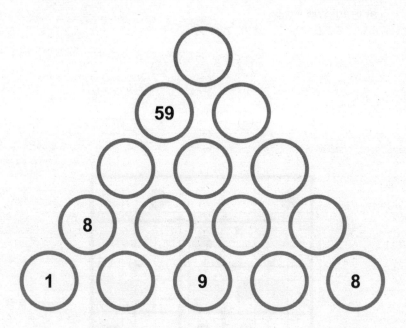

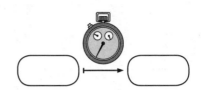

66

One to Nine

Using the numbers below, complete these six equations
(three reading across and three reading downwards).
Every number is used once.

1   2   3

4   5   6

7   8   9

	x		–		=	5
+		x		+		
	x	6	+		=	15
x		+		–		
	–		x		=	6
=		=		=		
40		23		14		

Number Crunch

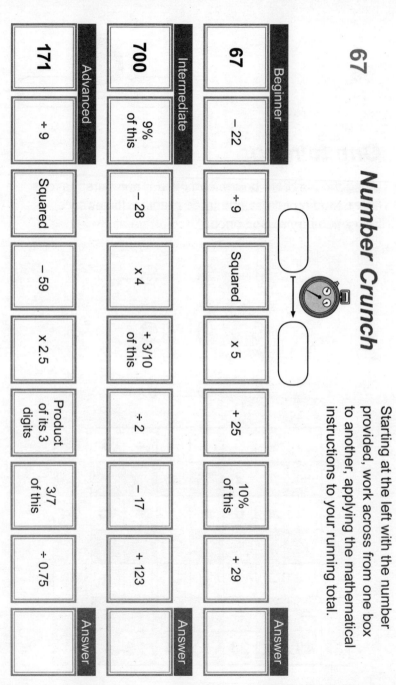

Starting at the left with the number provided, work across from one box to another, applying the mathematical instructions to your running total.

Beginner

67	− 22	÷ 9	Squared	× 5	+ 25	10% of this	+ 29	Answer

Intermediate

700	9% of this	− 28	× 4	+ 3/10 of this	÷ 2	− 17	+ 123	Answer

Advanced

171	÷ 9	Squared	− 59	× 2.5	Product of its 3 digits	3/7 of this	÷ 0.75	Answer

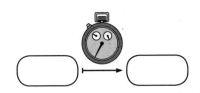

Summing Up

Arrange one of each of the four given numbers, as well as one each of the symbols – (minus), x (times) and + (plus) in every row and column to arrive at the answer at the end of the row or column, making the calculations in the order in which they appear.

3   4

7   9

9	–	3	+	4	x	7	=	70
x						–		
							=	96
						x		
							=	64
							=	40
=		=		=		=		
32		86		70		25		

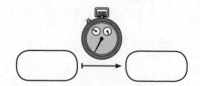

Isolate

Draw walls to partition the grid into areas (some walls are already drawn in for you). Each area must contain two circles, area sizes must match those shown by the numbers next to the grid and each '+' must be linked to at least two walls.

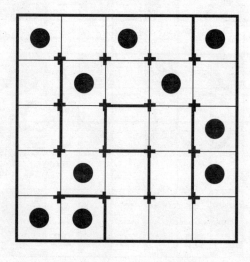

Pyramid Plus

The number in each circle is the sum of the two numbers below it. Just work out the missing numbers in every circle!

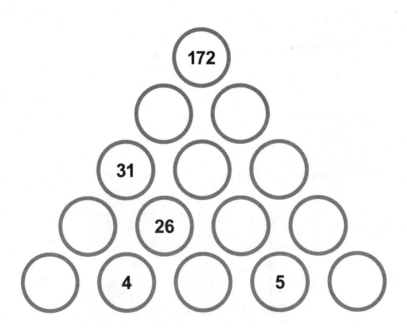

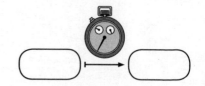

One to Nine

Using the numbers below, complete these six equations (three reading across and three reading downwards). Every number is used once.

1 2 3

4 5 6

7 8 9

	x		−	9	=	1
+		x		−		
	x		+		=	10
−		+		x		
	+		x		=	80
=		=		=		
3		9		48		

72

Number Crunch

Starting at the left with the number provided, work across from one box to another, applying the mathematical instructions to your running total.

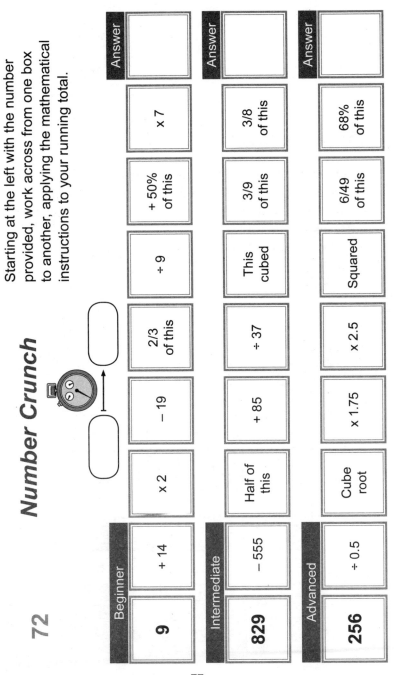

Beginner								Answer
9	+ 14	x 2	− 19	2/3 of this	÷ 9	+ 50% of this	x 7	

Intermediate								Answer
829	− 555	Half of this	+ 85	÷ 37	This cubed	3/9 of this	3/8 of this	

Advanced								Answer
256	÷ 0.5	Cube root	x 1.75	x 2.5	Squared	6/49 of this	68% of this	

Summing Up

Arrange one of each of the four given numbers, as well as one each of the symbols − (minus), x (times) and + (plus) in every row and column to arrive at the answer at the end of the row or column, making the calculations in the order in which they appear.

3 4

6 9

4	+	3	x	9	−	6	=	57
6	−						=	45
							=	15
							=	25
=		=		=		=		
18		33		60		41		

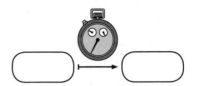

Isolate

Draw walls to partition the grid into areas (some walls are already drawn in for you). Each area must contain two circles, area sizes must match those shown by the numbers next to the grid and each '+' must be linked to at least two walls.

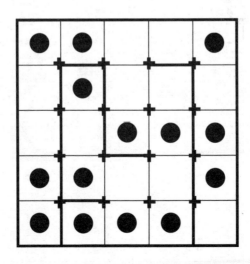

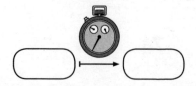

Pyramid Plus

The number in each circle is the sum of the two numbers below it. Just work out the missing numbers in every circle!

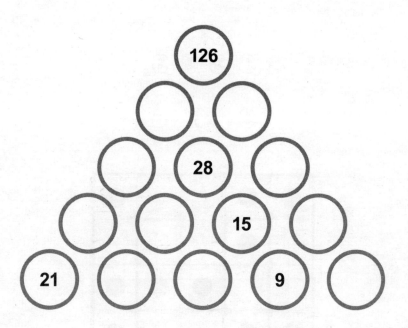

76

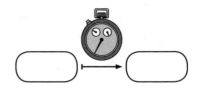

One to Nine

Using the numbers below, complete these six equations
(three reading across and three reading downwards).
Every number is used once.

1   2   3

4   5   6

7   8   9

	−		+		=	12
−		+		x		
	+	7	x		=	50
+		x		−		
	x		+		=	20
=		=		=		
8		48		12		

81

Number Crunch

Starting at the left with the number provided, work across from one box to another, applying the mathematical instructions to your running total.

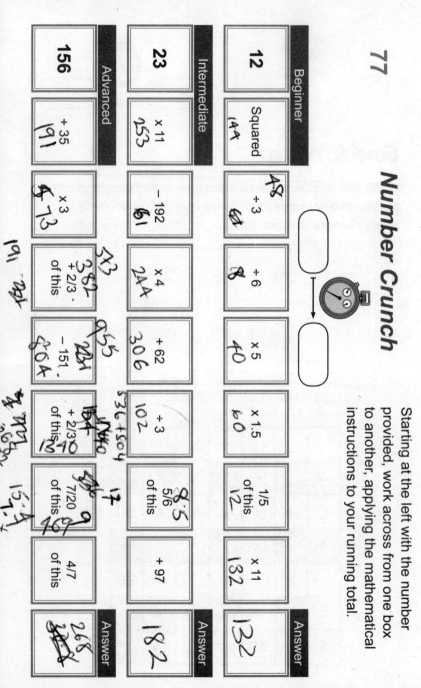

Beginner

| 12 | Squared *144* | ÷ 3 *48* | ÷ 6 *8* | × 5 *40* | × 1.5 *60* | 1/5 of this *12* | × 11 *132* | Answer *132* |

Intermediate

| 23 | × 11 *253* | − 192 *61* | × 4 *244* | + 62 *306* | ÷ 3 *102* | 5/6 of this *85* | + 97 | Answer *182* |

Advanced

| 156 | + 35 *191* | × 3 *573* | + 2/3 of this *382* | − 151 *864* | + 2/3 of this *1310* | 7/20 of this *167* | 4/7 of this | Answer *268* |

(handwritten working: 191 221, 255 221, 636+504, 17, 191, 2655, 1310, 151·4, 15·4, 7·7 ...)

Summing Up

Arrange one of each of the four given numbers, as well as one each of the symbols – (minus), x (times) and + (plus) in every row and column to arrive at the answer at the end of the row or column, making the calculations in the order in which they appear.

7	+	3	x	8	–	2	=	78
							=	12
			–		x		=	64
				3			=	25
=		=		=		=		
23		19		27		33		

Isolate

Draw walls to partition the grid into areas (some walls are already drawn in for you). Each area must contain two circles, area sizes must match those shown by the numbers next to the grid and each '+' must be linked to at least two walls.

2 3 3

5 6 6

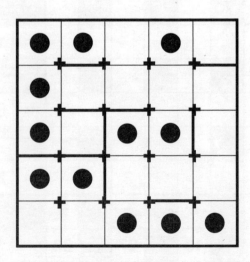

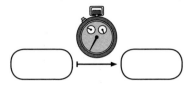

Pyramid Plus

The number in each circle is the sum of the two numbers below it. Just work out the missing numbers in every circle!

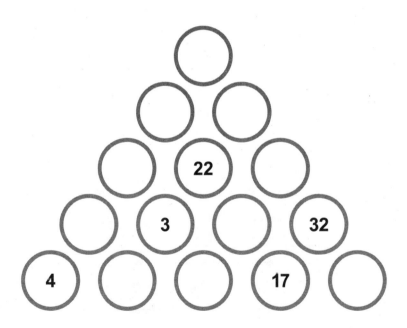

One to Nine

Using the numbers below, complete these six equations (three reading across and three reading downwards). Every number is used once.

$$1 \quad 2 \quad 3$$

$$4 \quad 5 \quad 6$$

$$7 \quad 8 \quad 9$$

	−		x		=	16
+		x		−		
	+		x		=	12
−		+		x		
	x		−	6	=	21
=		=		=		
8		19		42		

Number Crunch

Starting at the left with the number provided, work across from one box to another, applying the mathematical instructions to your running total.

82

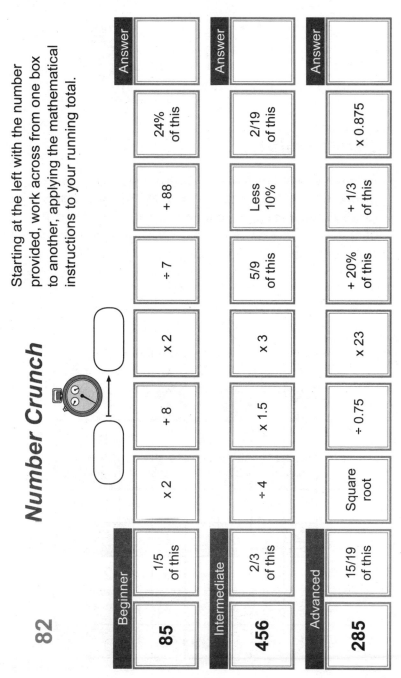

Beginner							Answer
85	1/5 of this	x 2	+ 8	x 2	÷ 7	+ 88	24% of this	

Intermediate							Answer
456	2/3 of this	÷ 4	x 1.5	x 3	5/9 of this	Less 10%	2/19 of this	

Advanced							Answer
285	15/19 of this	Square root	÷ 0.75	x 23	+ 20% of this	+ 1/3 of this	x 0.875	

Summing Up

Arrange one of each of the four given numbers, as well as one each of the symbols – (minus), x (times) and + (plus) in every row and column to arrive at the answer at the end of the row or column, making the calculations in the order in which they appear.

1   4
6   9

4	+	6	–	1	x	9	=	81
				6			=	11
							=	19
9							=	34
=		=		=		=		
27		57		59		36		

84

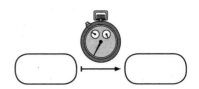

Isolate

Draw walls to partition the grid into areas (some walls are already drawn in for you). Each area must contain two circles, area sizes must match those shown by the numbers next to the grid and each '+' must be linked to at least two walls.

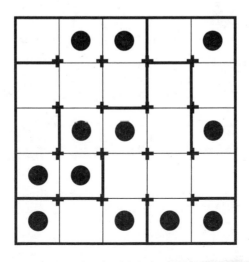

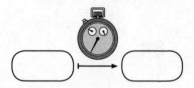

Pyramid Plus

The number in each circle is the sum of the two numbers below it. Just work out the missing numbers in every circle!

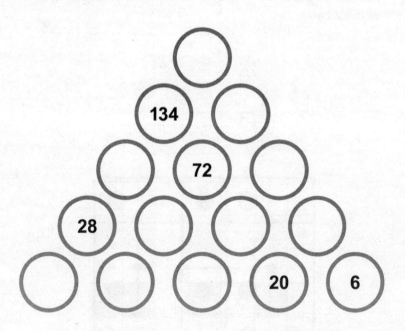

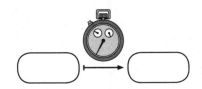

One to Nine

Using the numbers below, complete these six equations
(three reading across and three reading downwards).
Every number is used once.

$$1 \quad 2 \quad 3$$

$$4 \quad 5 \quad 6$$

$$7 \quad 8 \quad 9$$

	x	7	+		=	11
+		+		x		
	x		−		=	42
−		x		+		
	+		x		=	64
=		=		=		
4		96		20		

Number Crunch

Starting at the left with the number provided, work across from one box to another, applying the mathematical instructions to your running total.

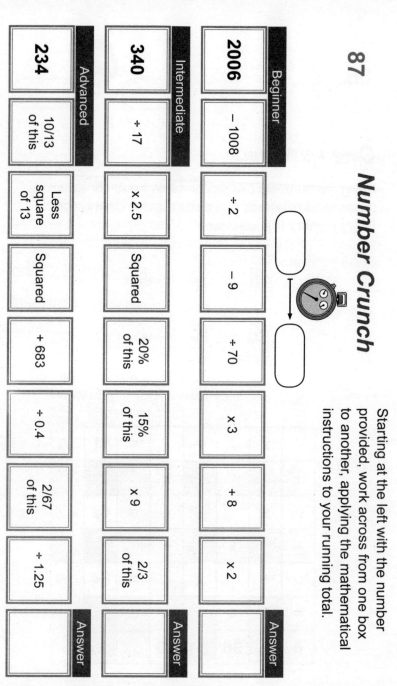

Beginner

| 2006 | − 1008 | ÷ 2 | − 9 | ÷ 70 | × 3 | + 8 | × 2 | Answer |

Intermediate

| 340 | ÷ 17 | × 2.5 | Squared | 20% of this | 15% of this | × 9 | 2/3 of this | Answer |

Advanced

| 234 | 10/13 of this | Less square of 13 | Squared | + 683 | ÷ 0.4 | 2/67 of this | ÷ 1.25 | Answer |

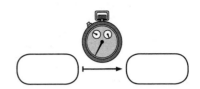

Summing Up

Arrange one of each of the four given numbers, as well as one each of the symbols – (minus), x (times) and + (plus) in every row and column to arrive at the answer at the end of the row or column, making the calculations in the order in which they appear.

3	+	8	–	7	x	5	=	20
							=	40
		x						
				5			=	42
							=	16
=		=		=		=		
14		8		54		57		

93

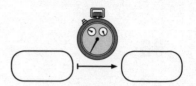

Isolate

Draw walls to partition the grid into areas (some walls are already drawn in for you). Each area must contain two circles, area sizes must match those shown by the numbers next to the grid and each '+' must be linked to at least two walls.

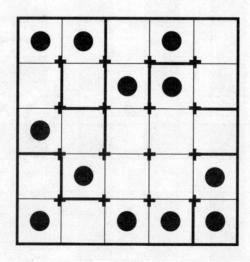

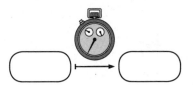

Pyramid Plus

The number in each circle is the sum of the two numbers below it. Just work out the missing numbers in every circle!

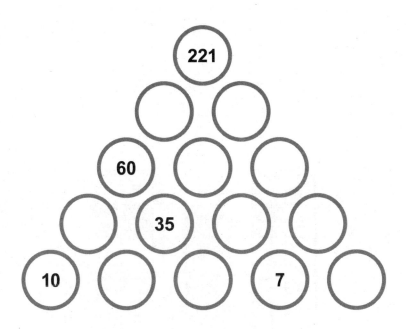

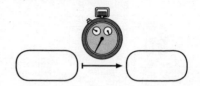

One to Nine

Using the numbers below, complete these six equations (three reading across and three reading downwards). Every number is used once.

1 2 3

4 5 6

7 8 9

	−		x		=	35
x		+		−		
	+		x		=	11
−		x		x		
	x		−	6	=	18
=		=		=		
33		72		24		

Number Crunch

Starting at the left with the number provided, work across from one box to another, applying the mathematical instructions to your running total.

92

Beginner

| 19 | − 11 | × 4 | × 3 | − 18 | + 3 | ÷ 9 | Square root | Answer |

Intermediate

| 73 | − 37 | Square root | × 13 | 1/3 of this | 6/13 of this | 1 5/6 of this | × 11 | Answer |

Advanced

| 91 | × 11 | − 869 | 5/6 of this | + 30% of this | ÷ 0.25 | + 38 | 80% of this | Answer |

Summing Up

Arrange one of each of the four given numbers, as well as one each of the symbols – (minus), x (times) and + (plus) in every row and column to arrive at the answer at the end of the row or column, making the calculations in the order in which they appear.

4   6

7   9

9	–	4	x	7	+	6	=	41
						x		
							=	53
–								
							=	31
	–				x		=	40
=		=		=		=		
77		35		81		37		

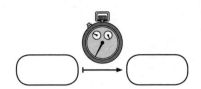

Isolate

Draw walls to partition the grid into areas (some walls are already drawn in for you). Each area must contain two circles, area sizes must match those shown by the numbers next to the grid and each '+' must be linked to at least two walls.

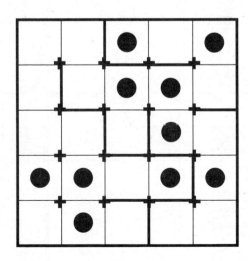

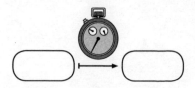

Pyramid Plus

The number in each circle is the sum of the two numbers below it. Just work out the missing numbers in every circle!

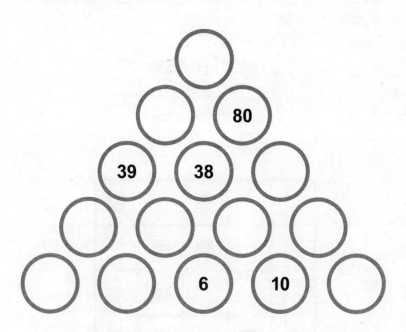

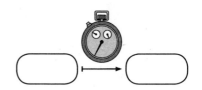

One to Nine

Using the numbers below, complete these six equations
(three reading across and three reading downwards).
Every number is used once.

1   2   3

4   5   6

7   8   9

1	+		x		=	45
x		+		−		
	x		−		=	40
+		x		+		
	−		+		=	10
=		=		=		
12		30		15		

Number Crunch

Starting at the left with the number provided, work across from one box to another, applying the mathematical instructions to your running total.

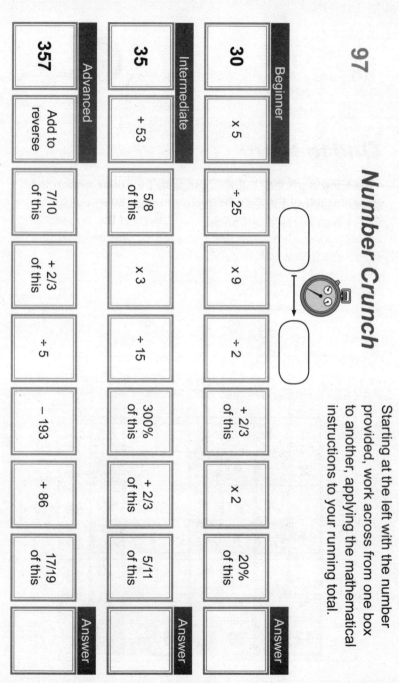

Beginner

| 30 | × 5 | ÷ 25 | × 9 | ÷ 2 | + 2/3 of this | × 2 | 20% of this | Answer |

Intermediate

| 35 | + 53 | 5/8 of this | × 3 | ÷ 15 | 300% of this | + 2/3 of this | 5/11 of this | Answer |

Advanced

| 357 | Add to reverse | 7/10 of this | + 2/3 of this | ÷ 5 | − 193 | + 86 | 17/19 of this | Answer |

98

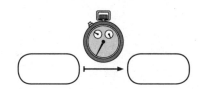

Summing Up

Arrange one of each of the four given numbers, as well
as one each of the symbols – (minus), x (times) and +
(plus) in every row and column to arrive at the answer
at the end of the row or column, making the calculations
in the order in which they appear.

2   5

6   8

6	x	2	+	5	–	8	=	9
				–				
							=	12
			x				=	86
		–						
							=	15
=		=		=		=		
18		8		30		20		

103

Isolate

Draw walls to partition the grid into areas (some walls are already drawn in for you). Each area must contain two circles, area sizes must match those shown by the numbers next to the grid and each '+' must be linked to at least two walls.

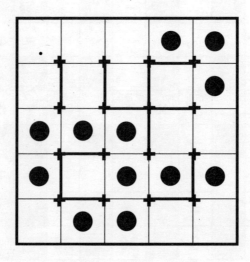

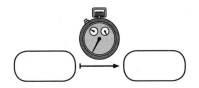

Pyramid Plus

The number in each circle is the sum of the two numbers below it. Just work out the missing numbers in every circle!

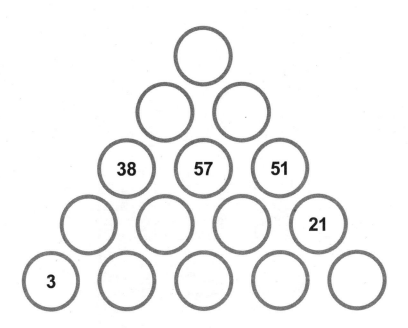

101

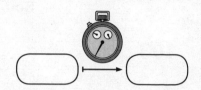

One to Nine

Using the numbers below, complete these six equations
(three reading across and three reading downwards).
Every number is used once.

1   2   3

4   5   6

7   8   9

	+		x		=	22
−		+		x		
	x		+		=	14
x		−		+		
	+		−	3	=	11
=		=		=		
15		4		19		

106

Solutions

1

4	x	6	–	9	=	15
+		x		+		
8	–	1	x	3	=	21
–		+		x		
2	x	5	+	7	=	17
=		=		=		
10		11		84		

3

3	+	8	x	2	–	7	=	15
–		–		+		+		
2	+	7	–	3	x	8	=	48
+		+		x		x		
7	–	3	+	8	x	2	=	24
x		x		–		–		
8	x	2	–	7	+	3	=	12
=		=		=		=		
64		8		33		27		

2

Beginner:
94 – 16 = 78, 78 ÷ 2 = 39, 39 ÷ 3 x 2 = 26, 26 + 14 = 40, 40 ÷ 5 x 3 = 24, 24 x 3 = 72, 72 + 28 = 100
Intermediate:
2222 ÷ 11 = 202, 150% of 202 = 303, 303 + 30 = 333, 333 ÷ 37 x 5 = 45, 45 ÷ 15 = 3, 3 ÷ 3 x 2 = 2, 2 x 86 = 172
Advanced:
247 ÷ 13 x 3 = 57, 57 ÷ 19 x 5 = 15, 15 x 35 = 525, 525 ÷ 21 x 5 = 125, cube root of 125 = 5, 5 x 1.4 = 7, 7 x 45 = 315

4

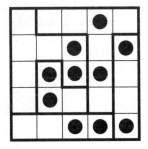

5

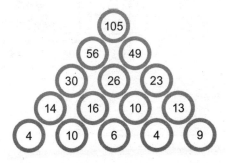

Solutions

6

8	–	1	x	5	=	35
+		+		x		
2	x	9	+	3	=	21
–		x		+		
4	x	6	–	7	=	17
=		=		=		
6		60		22		

7

Beginner:
$47 - 38 = 9$, $9^2 = 81$, $81 \div 3 = 27$, $27 + 9 = 36$, square root of $36 = 6$, $6 \times 7 = 42$, $42 - 18 = 24$

Intermediate:
$55 \div 11 \times 4 = 20$, $20 \times 1.75 = 35$, $35 \div 7 \times 2 = 10$, 400% of 10 $= 40$, $40 + 47 = 87$, $87 \div 3 \times 2 = 58$, $58 \div 0.5 = 116$

Advanced:
$33 \times 25 = 825$, $825 \div 3 \times 2 = 550$, $550 \div 11 \times 9 = 450$, 28% of $450 = 126$, $126 \div 14 \times 5 = 45$, $45 + 89 = 134$, $134 \div 0.25 = 536$

8

5	+	9	x	3	–	6	=	36
–		x		x		+		
3	x	5	–	6	+	9	=	18
x		–		+		x		
9	+	6	x	5	–	3	=	72
+		+		–		–		
6	–	3	x	9	+	5	=	32
=		=		=		=		
24		42		14		40		

9

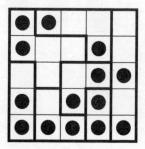

10

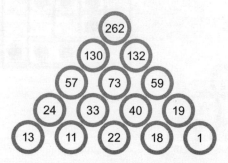

108

Solutions

11

2	+	7	−	5	=	4
+		−		x		
6	x	3	−	8	=	10
x		+		−		
9	−	1	x	4	=	32
=		=		=		
72		5		36		

13

6	x	9	−	4	+	7	=	57
−		+		x		−		
4	+	7	−	9	x	6	=	12
x		−		−		x		
7	−	4	x	6	+	9	=	27
+		x		+		+		
9	+	6	−	7	x	4	=	32
=		=		=		=		
23		72		37		13		

12

Beginner:
$6 ÷ 3 = 2$, $2^2 = 4$, $4 \times 8 = 32$,
$32 ÷ 8 \times 3 = 12$, $12 + 98 = 110$,
10% of $110 = 11$, $11 \times 12 = 132$
Intermediate:
$59 \times 3 = 177$, $177 − 114 = 63$,
$63 + 21 = 84$, $84 ÷ 12 \times 5 = 35$,
$35 ÷ 7 \times 3 = 15$, $15 \times 13 = 195$,
$195 + 85 = 280$
Advanced:
$578 ÷ 2 = 289$, square root of
$289 = 17$, $17 + 68 = 85$, 80% of
$85 = 68$, $68 \times 1.75 = 119$, $119 \times 2 = 238$, $238 − 109 = 129$

14

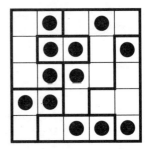

15

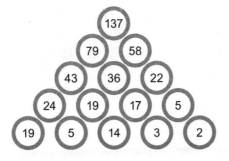

Solutions

16

5	+	4	x	7	=	63
−		x		+		
3	x	9	−	1	=	26
x		+		x		
2	x	6	+	8	=	20
=		=		=		
4		42		64		

17

Beginner:
51 ÷ 3 = 17, 17 + 18 = 35, 35 ÷ 5 x 4 = 28, 28 ÷ 4 x 3 = 21, 21 + 37 = 58, 58 − 49 = 9, 9 x 8 = 72
Intermediate:
32 x 5 = 160, 160 + 16 = 176, 176 ÷ 4 = 44, 44 ÷ 11 x 5 = 20, 20 x 4.5 = 90, 90 ÷ 5 = 18, 18 x 3 = 54
Advanced:
240 ÷ 40 x 9 = 54, 54 x 7 = 378, 378 ÷ 18 x 11 = 231, 231 ÷ 1.5 = 154, 154 x 5 = 770, 770 x 1.6 = 1232, 1232 + 2321 = 3553

18

2	+	8	x	5	−	4	=	46
x		−		−		+		
5	x	4	−	2	+	8	=	26
−		+		x		x		
4	+	2	x	8	−	5	=	43
+		x		+		−		
8	x	5	+	4	−	2	=	42
=		=		=		=		
14		30		28		58		

19

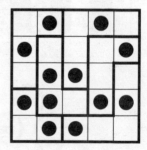

20

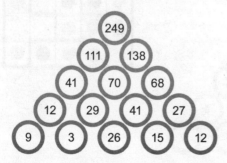

Solutions

21

8	x	3	+	6	=	30
−		+		x		
5	+	2	x	7	=	49
+		x		−		
1	+	9	x	4	=	40
=		=		=		
4		45		38		

22

Beginner:
$10 \div 5 \times 2 = 4$, $4^2 = 16$, $16 \div 4 \times 3 = 12$, $12 \times 9 = 108$, $108 \div 6 = 18$, $18 + 48 = 66$, $66 \div 3 = 22$
Intermediate:
$99 \div 9 \times 5 = 55$, $55 \div 11 \times 5 = 25$, square root of $25 = 5$, $5 + 1 = 6$, $6 + 5 = 11$, $11^2 = 121$, $121 \times 3 = 363$
Advanced:
$161 \div 7 \times 4 = 92$, $92 + 749 = 841$, $841 \times 3 = 2523$, $2523 + 1682 = 4205$, $4205 \div 5 = 841$, $841 + 92 = 933$, $933 − 719 = 214$

23

3	+	7	−	9	x	6	=	6
x		−		+		x		
9	−	3	x	6	+	7	=	43
+		x		−		−		
6	x	9	+	7	−	3	=	58
−		+		x		+		
7	−	6	+	3	x	9	=	36
=		=		=		=		
26		42		24		48		

24

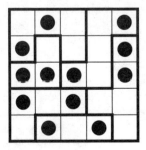

25

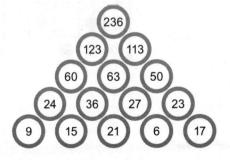

111

Solutions

26

4	+	2	x	5	=	30
+		x		−		
6	+	9	−	3	=	12
−		+		x		
8	−	1	x	7	=	49
=		=		=		
2		19		14		

27

Beginner:
56 + 15 = 71, 71 − 7 = 64, 64 ÷ 4 = 16, square root of 16 = 4, 4 + 69 = 73, 73 − 14 = 59, 59 + 23 = 82

Intermediate:
127 + 43 = 170, 170 + 34 = 204, 204 ÷ 4 = 51, 51 ÷ 3 = 17, 17 + 283 = 300, 31% of 300 = 93, 93 − 67 = 26

Advanced:
76^2 = 5776, 5776 ÷ 8 x 5 = 3610, 3610 ÷ 10 x 7 = 2527, 2527 ÷ 7 x 2 = 722, 722 + 82 = 804, 804 ÷ 4 x 3 = 603, 603 ÷ 9 x 7 = 469

28

6	+	4	x	8	−	3	=	77
−		+		−		x		
3	x	8	−	4	+	6	=	26
x		x		x		+		
4	−	3	x	6	+	8	=	14
+		−		+		−		
8	+	6	−	3	x	4	=	44
=		=		=		=		
20		30		27		22		

29

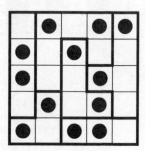

30

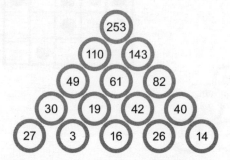

112

Solutions

31

8	–	6	x	4	=	8
+		x		+		
1	+	3	x	9	=	36
x		+		x		
5	x	7	–	2	=	33
=		=		=		
45		25		26		

32

Beginner:
90 ÷ 5 = 18, 18 ÷ 3 x 2 = 12, 12 ÷ 4 x 3 = 9, 9 x 8 = 72, 72 + 28 = 100, 100 + 20 = 120, 120 ÷ 3 = 40

Intermediate:
32 ÷ 8 x 7 = 28, 125% of 28 = 35, 35 x 7 = 245, 245 + 27 = 272, 272 ÷ 4 = 68, 68 ÷ 4 = 17, 17 + 84 = 101

Advanced:
5 x 5 x 9 = 225, square root of 225 = 15, 15 x 39 = 585, 585 ÷ 9 x 4 + 585 = 845, 845 ÷ 5 = 169, 169 – 77 = 92, 92 x 3 + (92 ÷ 4 x 3) = 345

33

5	+	9	x	2	–	7	=	21
–		–		+		+		
2	x	5	–	7	+	9	=	12
+		x		x		x		
7	–	2	x	9	+	5	=	50
x		+		–		–		
9	+	7	–	5	x	2	=	22
=		=		=		=		
90		15		76		78		

34

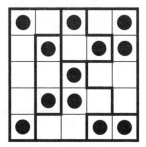

35

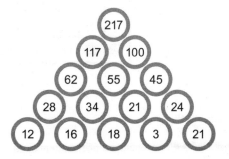

113

Solutions

36

9	−	3	x	8	=	48
+		x		−		
2	+	6	x	5	=	40
x		−		x		
7	+	4	−	1	=	10
=		=		=		
77		14		3		

37

Beginner:
1001 x 5 = 5005, 5005 − 355 = 4650, 10% of 4650 = 465, 465 ÷ 5 = 93, 93 ÷ 3 = 31, 31 + 29 = 60, 60 ÷ 4 = 15
Intermediate:
19 x 4 = 76, 76 − 18 = 58, 58 + 37 = 95, 95 ÷ 19 x 16 = 80, 20% of 80 = 16, square root of 16 = 4, 4 x 23 = 92
Advanced:
425 ÷ 17 x 11 = 275, 275 ÷ 11 x 5 = 125, 125 x 0.4 = 50, 320% of 50 = 160, 160 ÷ 32 x 23 = 115, 115 ÷ 23 x 18 = 90, 90 ÷ 0.3 = 300

38

4	+	7	x	3	−	8	=	25
x		−		+		−		
8	−	3	x	7	+	4	=	39
−		x		x		+		
3	x	4	−	8	+	7	=	11
+		+		−		x		
7	x	8	+	4	−	3	=	57
=		=		=		=		
36		24		76		33		

39

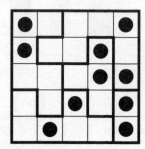

40

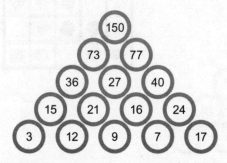

Solutions

41

4	+	1	x	7	=	35
x		+		–		
6	+	8	–	2	=	12
–		x		+		
3	x	5	+	9	=	24
=		=		=		
21		45		14		

42

Beginner:
31 – 15 = 16, 16 + 4 = 20, 20 + 18 = 38, 38 ÷ 2 = 19, 19 – 11 = 8, 8² = 64, 64 + 146 = 210
Intermediate:
1215 ÷ 5 = 243, 243 ÷ 27 = 9, 9 ÷ 9 x 5 + 9 = 14, 14 ÷ 7 x 3 = 6, 6 + 4 = 10, 950% of 10 = 95, 95 + 36 = 131
Advanced:
36 + 20 = 56, 56 x 1.375 = 77, 77 x 7 = 539, 539 – 33 = 506, 506 ÷ 22 x 19 = 437, 437 – 91 = 346, 346 x 2.5 = 865

43

5	x	8	+	2	–	6	=	36
+		–		x		+		
6	–	2	x	5	+	8	=	28
x		+		–		x		
8	–	5	+	6	x	2	=	18
–		x		+		–		
2	+	6	x	8	–	5	=	59
=		=		=		=		
86		66		12		23		

44

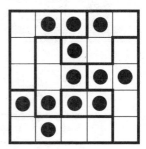

45

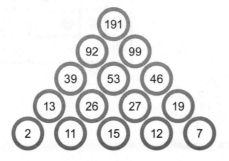

115

Solutions

46

3	x	6	–	9	=	9
+		–		+		
2	+	5	x	7	=	49
x		x		x		
8	–	1	+	4	=	11
=		=		=		
40		1		64		

47

Beginner:
60% of 200 = 120, 120 ÷ 4 = 30, 30 + 10 = 40, 40 x 4 = 160, 160 ÷ 20 = 8, 8 x 11 = 88, 88 – 42 = 46

Intermediate:
488 ÷ 8 = 61, 61 – 17 = 44, 44 ÷ 11 x 5 + 44 = 64, cube root of 64 = 4, 4 x 26 = 104, 104 ÷ 4 x 3 = 78, 78 ÷ 3 = 26

Advanced:
92 ÷ 23 x 17 = 68, 68 ÷ 17 x 4 = 16, 16^2 = 256, 256 x 0.375 = 96, 96 ÷ 16 x 3 = 18, 18^2 = 324, 324 ÷ 36 x 23 = 207

48

5	+	7	–	2	x	9	=	90
–		+		x		–		
2	x	5	+	9	–	7	=	12
x		x		–		+		
9	–	2	x	7	+	5	=	54
+		–		+		x		
7	+	9	x	5	–	2	=	78
=		=		=		=		
34		15		16		14		

49

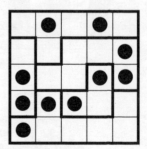

50

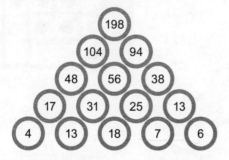

Solutions

51

3	+	7	x	1	=	10
x		−		+		
6	−	5	x	9	=	9
+		x		x		
8	x	4	+	2	=	34
=		=		=		
26		8		20		

52

Beginner:
95 + 18 = 113, 113 − 72 = 41, 41 x 2 = 82, 82 x 1.5 = 123, 123 − 16 = 107, 107 − 17 = 90, 90 x 4 = 360
Intermediate:
49 x 2 = 98, 98 − 19 = 79, 79 x 3 = 237, 237 − 109 = 128, 128 ÷ 8 = 16, 16 x 1.5 = 24, 24 ÷ 8 x 5 = 15
Advanced:
59 x 4 = 236, 236 ÷ 4 x 3 + 236 = 413, 413 − 78 = 335, 335 x 0.2 = 67, 67 + 233 = 300, 61% of 300 = 183, 183 ÷ 3 x 2 + 183 = 305

53

5	−	3	+	8	x	7	=	70
+		x		−		+		
8	+	7	−	5	x	3	=	30
x		−		x		−		
3	x	8	+	7	−	5	=	26
−		+		+		x		
7	−	5	x	3	+	8	=	14
=		=		=		=		
32		18		24		40		

54

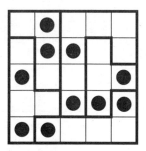

55

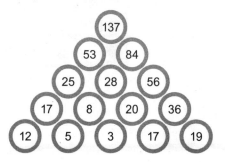

117

Solutions

56

4	x	9	−	6	=	30
x		+		−		
3	+	7	x	1	=	10
+		−		+		
8	−	5	x	2	=	6
=		=		=		
20		11		7		

57

Beginner:
2^2 = 4, 4 x 9 = 36, square root of 36 = 6, 6 x 7 = 42, 42 ÷ 3 = 14, 14 + 8 = 22, 22 + 38 = 60
Intermediate:
291 + 49 = 340, 20% of 340 = 68, 68 ÷ 4 = 17, 17 x 7 = 119, 119 x 2 = 238, 238 − 190 = 48, 48 ÷ 3 x 2 + 48 = 80
Advanced:
72 ÷ 12 x 7 = 42, 300% of 42 = 126, 126 ÷ 14 x 11 = 99, 99 ÷ 0.3 = 330, 330 ÷ 11 x 10 = 300, 94% of 300 = 282, 282 ÷ 3 x 2 = 188

58

9	−	3	+	1	x	8	=	56
+		x		+		−		
1	x	9	−	8	+	3	=	4
x		−		x		+		
3	+	8	x	9	−	1	=	98
−		+		−		x		
8	−	1	+	3	x	9	=	90
=		=		=		=		
22		20		78		54		

59

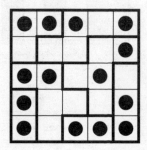

60

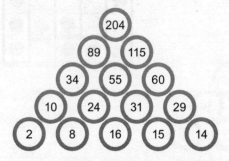

Solutions

61

9	–	2	+	7	=	14
–		+		–		
4	+	8	–	3	=	9
x		x		+		
1	x	6	+	5	=	11
=		=		=		
5		60		9		

62

Beginner:
35 ÷ 5 = 7, 7 + 27 = 34, 34 x 2 = 68, 68 ÷ 4 = 17, 17 – 8 = 9, square root of 9 = 3, 3 x 15 = 45

Intermediate:
29 – 14 = 15, 15² = 225, 225 ÷ 3 = 75, 75 ÷ 3 x 2 + 75 = 125, 125 ÷ 5 x 4 = 100, 67% of 100 = 67, 67 + 88 = 155

Advanced:
43 x 7 = 301, 301 + 199 = 500, 69% of 500 = 345, 345 ÷ 15 x 9 = 207, 207 ÷ 23 x 17 = 153, 153 ÷ 9 x 4 = 68, 68 x 7 = 476

63

3	x	7	–	5	+	2	=	18
+		–		x		+		
5	–	2	x	7	+	3	=	24
x		x		–		x		
2	+	5	x	3	–	7	=	14
–		+		+		–		
7	+	3	x	2	–	5	=	15
=		=		=		=		
9		28		34		30		

64

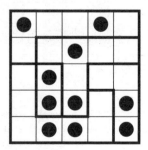

65

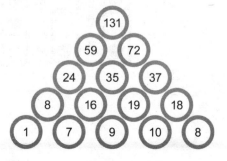

Solutions

66

4	x	3	–	7	=	5
+		x		+		
1	x	6	+	9	=	15
x		+		–		
8	–	5	x	2	=	6
=		=		=		
40		23		14		

67

Beginner:
67 – 22 = 45, 45 ÷ 9 = 5, 5² = 25, 25 x 5 = 125, 125 + 25 = 150, 10% of 150 = 15, 15 + 29 = 44

Intermediate:
9% of 700 = 63, 63 – 28 = 35, 35 x 4 = 140, 140 + 42 = 182, 182 ÷ 2 = 91, 91 – 17 = 74, 74 + 123 = 197

Advanced:
171 ÷ 9 = 19, 19² = 361, 361 – 59 = 302, 302 x 2.5 = 755, 7 x 5 x 5 = 175, 175 ÷ 7 x 3 = 75, 75 ÷ 0.75 = 100

68

9	–	3	+	4	x	7	=	70
x		+		+		–		
4	+	7	x	9	–	3	=	96
–		x		–		x		
7	x	9	–	3	+	4	=	64
+		–		x		+		
3	+	4	x	7	–	9	=	40
=		=		=		=		
32		86		70		25		

69

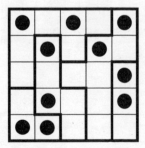

70

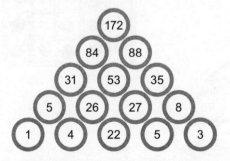

Solutions

71

2	x	5	–	9	=	1
+		x		–		
7	x	1	+	3	=	10
–		+		x		
6	+	4	x	8	=	80
=		=		=		
3		9		48		

72

Beginner:
$9 + 14 = 23$, $23 \times 2 = 46$, $46 - 19 = 27$, $27 \div 3 \times 2 = 18$, $18 \div 9 = 2$, $2 + 1 = 3$, $3 \times 7 = 21$
Intermediate:
$829 - 555 = 274$, $274 \div 2 = 137$, $137 + 85 = 222$, $222 \div 37 = 6$, $6^3 = 216$, $216 \div 9 \times 3 = 72$, $72 \div 8 \times 3 = 27$
Advanced:
$256 \div 0.5 = 512$, cube root of $512 = 8$, $8 \times 1.75 = 14$, $14 \times 2.5 = 35$, $35^2 = 1225$, $1225 \div 49 \times 6 = 150$, 68% of $150 = 102$

73

4	+	3	x	9	–	6	=	57
x		+		–		+		
6	–	4	+	3	x	9	=	45
–		x		+		x		
9	–	6	x	4	+	3	=	15
+		–		x		–		
3	x	9	–	6	+	4	=	25
=		=		=		=		
18		33		60		41		

74

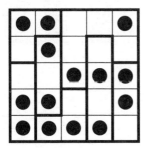

75

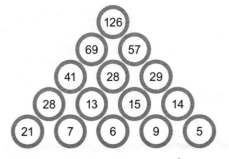

Solutions

76

9	−	1	+	4	=	12
−		+		x		
3	+	7	x	5	=	50
+		x		−		
2	x	6	+	8	=	20
=		=		=		
8		48		12		

77

Beginner:
$12^2 = 144$, $144 ÷ 3 = 48$, $48 ÷ 6 = 8$, $8 \times 5 = 40$, $40 \times 1.5 = 60$, $60 ÷ 5 = 12$, $12 \times 11 = 132$

Intermediate:
$23 \times 11 = 253$, $253 − 192 = 61$, $61 \times 4 = 244$, $244 + 62 = 306$, $306 ÷ 3 = 102$, $102 ÷ 6 \times 5 = 85$, $85 + 97 = 182$

Advanced:
$156 + 35 = 191$, $191 \times 3 = 573$, $573 + 382 = 955$, $955 − 151 = 804$, $804 + 536 = 1340$, $1340 ÷ 20 \times 7 = 469$, $469 ÷ 7 \times 4 = 268$

78

7	+	3	x	8	−	2	=	78
−		x		+		+		
2	x	8	−	7	+	3	=	12
x		−		x		x		
3	+	7	−	2	x	8	=	64
+		+		−		−		
8	−	2	x	3	+	7	=	25
=		=		=		=		
23		19		27		33		

79

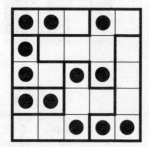

80

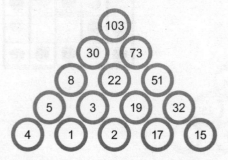

Solutions

81

4	−	2	x	8	=	16
+		x		−		
7	+	5	x	1	=	12
−		+		x		
3	x	9	−	6	=	21
=		=		=		
8		19		42		

82

Beginner:
85 ÷ 5 = 17, 17 x 2 = 34, 34 + 8 = 42, 42 x 2 = 84, 84 ÷ 7 = 12, 12 + 88 = 100, 24% of 100 = 24
Intermediate:
456 ÷ 3 x 2 = 304, 304 ÷ 4 = 76, 76 x 1.5 = 114, 114 x 3 = 342, 342 ÷ 9 x 5 = 190, 190 − 19 = 171, 171 ÷ 19 x 2 = 18
Advanced:
285 ÷ 19 x 15 = 225, square root of 225 = 15, 15 ÷ 0.75 = 20, 20 x 23 = 460, 460 + 92 = 552, 552 + 184 = 736, 736 x 0.875 = 644

83

4	+	6	−	1	x	9	=	81
−		x		+		−		
1	x	9	+	6	−	4	=	11
x		+		x		+		
6	−	4	x	9	+	1	=	19
+		−		−		x		
9	+	1	x	4	−	6	=	34
=		=		=		=		
27		57		59		36		

84

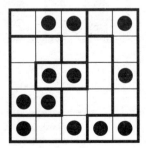

85

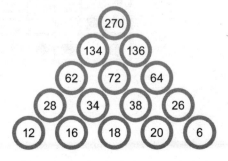

Solutions

86

1	x	7	+	4	=	11
+		+		x		
5	x	9	−	3	=	42
−		x		+		
2	+	6	x	8	=	64
=		=		=		
4		96		20		

87

Beginner:
2006 − 1008 = 998, 998 ÷ 2 = 499, 499 − 9 = 490, 490 ÷ 70 = 7, 7 x 3 = 21, 21 + 8 = 29, 29 x 2 = 58

Intermediate:
340 ÷ 17 = 20, 20 x 2.5 = 50, 50^2 = 2500, 20% of 2500 = 500, 15% of 500 = 75, 75 x 9 = 675, 675 ÷ 3 x 2 = 450

Advanced:
234 ÷ 13 x 10 = 180, 180 − 169 = 11, 11^2 = 121, 121 + 683 = 804, 804 ÷ 0.4 = 2010, 2010 ÷ 67 x 2 = 60, 60 ÷ 1.25 = 48

88

3	+	8	−	7	x	5	=	20
x		−		x		+		
5	x	7	+	8	−	3	=	40
+		x		−		x		
7	+	3	x	5	−	8	=	42
−		+		+		−		
8	−	5	x	3	+	7	=	16
=		=		=		=		
14		8		54		57		

89

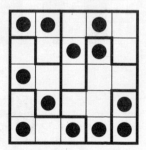

90

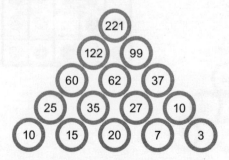

124

Solutions

91

9	–	2	x	5	=	35
x		+		–		
4	+	7	x	1	=	11
–		x		x		
3	x	8	–	6	=	18
=		=		=		
33		72		24		

92

Beginner:
19 – 11 = 8, 8 x 4 = 32, 32 x 3 = 96, 96 – 18 = 78, 78 + 3 = 81, 81 ÷ 9 = 9, square root of 9 = 3
Intermediate:
73 – 37 = 36, square root of 36 = 6, 6 x 13 = 78, 78 ÷ 3 = 26, 26 ÷ 13 x 6 = 12, 12 ÷ 6 x 5 + 12 = 22, 22 x 11 = 242
Advanced:
91 x 11 = 1001, 1001 – 869 = 132, 132 ÷ 6 x 5 = 110, 110 + 33 = 143, 143 ÷ 0.25 = 572, 572 + 38 = 610, 80% of 610 = 488

93

9	–	4	x	7	+	6	=	41
+		x		–		x		
6	+	9	x	4	–	7	=	53
–		–		+		–		
4	x	7	–	6	+	9	=	31
x		+		x		+		
7	–	6	+	9	x	4	=	40
=		=		=		=		
77		35		81		35		

94

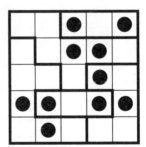

95

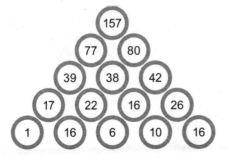

125

Solutions

96

1	+	4	x	9	=	45
x		+		−		
7	x	6	−	2	=	40
+		x		+		
5	−	3	+	8	=	10
=		=		=		
12		30		15		

97

Beginner:
30 x 5 = 150, 150 ÷ 25 = 6, 6 x 9 = 54, 54 ÷ 2 = 27, 27 + 18 = 45, 45 x 2 = 90, 20% of 90 = 18
Intermediate:
35 + 53 = 88, 88 ÷ 8 x 5 = 55, 55 x 3 = 165, 165 ÷ 15 = 11, 300% of 11 = 33, 33 + 22 = 55, 55 ÷ 11 x 5 = 25
Advanced:
357 + 753 = 1110, 1110 ÷ 10 x 7 = 777, 777 + 518 = 1295, 1295 ÷ 5 = 259, 259 − 193 = 66, 66 + 86 = 152, 152 ÷ 19 x 17 = 136

98

6	x	2	+	5	−	8	=	9
+		x		−		−		
8	−	5	x	2	+	6	=	12
−		+		x		+		
5	+	6	x	8	−	2	=	86
x		−		+		x		
2	x	8	−	6	+	5	=	15
=		=		=		=		
18		8		30		20		

99

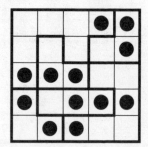

100

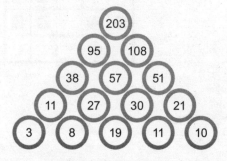

126

Solutions

101

4	+	7	x	2	=	22
–		+		x		
1	x	6	+	8	=	14
x		–		+		
5	+	9	–	3	=	11
=		=		=		
15		4		19		

BRILLIANT
MINDS

Bletchley Park played a vital role in the
course of British history. This vibrant
heritage attraction is open daily for
all to discover its secrets.

Visit bletchleypark.org.uk

BLETCHLEYPARK
Home of the Codebreakers